Battersea
Nocturne

South London Walks

Jon Newman

Thamesis
WALKIES

First published 2017
by Thamesis Publications
3b Webber Street
London SE1 8PZ
www.thamesispublications.co.uk

ISBN 978-0-9927045-4-4

Printed by Imprint Digital
www.imprintdigital.net
Design by Silbercow www.silbercow.co.uk

Supported using public funding by
ARTS COUNCIL
ENGLAND

THAMESIS WALKIES

Lovely Lambeth by Jon Newman (978-0-9927045-3-7)
Lost in Herne Hill by Jon Newman (978-0-9927045-5-1)

BATTERSEA NOCTURNE

James Abbot McNeill Whistler was an American born in 1834 in Lowell, Massachusetts. After considering and rejecting careers in the church, the army and as a surveyor he took himself to Paris in 1855 to train as an artist. After exhibiting there and travelling in Europe he came to London where he settled in Chelsea, living in a succession of riverside houses with views across the Thames to Battersea, a place which became the subject of many of his 'nocturnes' or twilight river landscapes. He was also a successful portrait painter and etcher, going back to Paris and travelling to Venice in later life before returning finally to Chelsea, where he died in 1903.

Battersea riverside today is an extreme example of 'regeneration', a renewal and rebuilding so complete that almost no traces of the area's earlier identity now remain. Along the mile and a half of the Thames Path between Battersea and Wandsworth bridges there remains just one building – the late-18th century church of St Mary's – which was built before 1980. The area's recent and rich industrial past exists only as fading memory, archive fragment and historic image. Of the latter it is the paintings and etchings of Whistler, who made the factories of Battersea the subject of many of his works of the 1860s and 1870s, that best provides the 'double-vision' which allow the bemused traveller passing through Battersea to re-connect with this earlier landscape.

James Whistler's statue in Battersea Bridge Gardens

Begin at the Cremorne Gardens on Lots Road, Chelsea

To consider Battersea's riverside through the eyes of Whistler, one must begin by going back to where he lived on the other side of the Thames. Whistler's several London houses were all in Chelsea and Cremorne Gardens – a place that he visited, painted and from where he was to compose many of his Battersea views – is as apt a starting point as any. Walter Greaves, the Chelsea boatman who lived on Cheyne Walk just along from Whistler and who served him as acolyte, artist apprentice and boat man, used to row Whistler down to Cremorne of a night, "where he loved to pick the pinks, blues and other colours out amongst the lights". Coming upon a view he would stop talking and start sketching, "just showing the position of the lights and the river banks and the bridges". Of the very small number of Whistler's paintings that can still be seen London's galleries, *Cremorne Lights* offers a twilight vista looking down the river from the middle of Battersea Bridge to the glittering lights of the pleasure gardens, while his *Nocturne in Black and Gold: The Firewheel* – also in Tate Britain – is an extraordinary pyrotechnic rendering of its night-time firework displays.

Today's rump of a small riverside gardens is a mere fragment of the larger and briefly famous Cremorne Pleasure Gardens which opened here in 1845 and closed in 1877; its grounds originally ran from the Thames back as far as Kings Road. Lord Cremorne acquired Chelsea Farm in 1778 and gave its enlarged and improved house its new name, making it into a society destination for Regency London visited by both King George III and the then Prince of Wales. By 1831 the house had passed from the family and the enterprising 'Baron De Beaufain' had turned it into a fashionable sports club for 'the cultivation of skilful and manly exercise' including shooting, swimming and fencing. The trace of that brief incarnation is the survival of the name of the neighbouring Stadium Street. Fifteen years later it was a pleasure gardens, modelled on those at Vauxhall and Ranelagh and, like them, increasingly given over to crowd-pleasing spectacle:

concerts, fireworks, balloon ascents and faux medieval tournaments. The early evening audience was respectable but after ten o'clock, rather like its rivals, "Cremorne is in the possession of Lost Women and their male friends and abettors".

In 1877 the moralists got Cremorne shut down and its gardens were quickly covered over with modest terraced streets. The grand cast iron gates seen in the park today and which date back to Lord Cremorne's days were rescued from what had subsequently become the Kings Road entrance to the Watney's brewery. They were restored and put up here when the park was re-landscaped in 1981-2. The Chelsea Borough Council's roll of honour for its World War One dead, moved here from Chelsea Old Town Hall, adds to a sense of the space as a repository for homeless artefacts. Yet despite the heritage imports, this revived garden has not yet accumulated memory or association; between the Versailles tubs of clipped evergreens and the palm trees, the un-memorialised wooden benches await their brass plaques.

Turn right out of Cremorne Gardens onto Lots Road and then turn immediately right onto Cheyne Walk. Walk along Cheyne Walk towards Battersea Bridge

Chelsea was the first high ground along the Thames west of Charing Cross. Tucked away on a bend in the river, it contrived to be both 'out-of' yet also 'on the edge-of' town, affordable to hard up writers like Leigh Hunt and Carlyle, who described it as like "living at the end of the world", and attractive to artists with an eye for its river- and sky-scapes. Turner was reported as saying to John Martin, when both artists were living on Cheyne Walk in the 1840s, "Here you see my study: sky and water. Are they not glorious? Here I have my lesson, night and day."

One still gets a sense of what drew such people to the place. The informal terrace of Cheyne Walk – with its views along the Thames, its multiple building lines and roof heights, its rag-bag of flat-fronts with their mansard-, balcony- and gable-afterthoughts and with its mix of bare brick, white stucco and salmon and magnolia paint-jobs – offers that increasingly rare London survival: an unplanned street that has grown over time into its space. By way of planned contrast the six towers of the World's End Estate (conceived in the early 1960s by Eric Lyons as the solution to the slum-clearance of West Chelsea but not completed until 1977) fill the skyline behind Cheyne Walk. Their intriguingly irregular polygonal structures, varying in height from 18 to 21 storeys, conceal their system-built concrete behind a cladding of brown brick. Whistler is name-checked among them: his is the most westerly of the towers.

Approaching Battersea Bridge, the house fronts of Cheyne Walk appear to become more heavily defended: walls rear up, fences over-top, front garden planting becomes denser and spikier and beneath the blue plaques memorialising earlier residents the houses retreat from the traffic behind locked gates. Would the twenty-first century equivalents of a contrarian like Carlyle, a campaigner like Pankhurst, or a poet like Swinburne either chose or afford to live amid the basement excavations, architectural make-overs and electronic surveillance and security of today's street?

Just before Battersea Bridge fork left onto the path into Battersea Bridge Gardens and the statue of James Whistler

If Chelsea is indeed one of the most obsessively memorialised areas of London with its blue-plaques along the Walk and its statues and memorials lurking among the bushes of the Embankment, then no one worked harder for his legacy here than James Whistler. When he came to settle in London in the 1860s, his choice of Chelsea was something of an act of non-compliance – a refusal to live in what was becoming the professional artists' enclave of Holland Park, "the Leighton settlement" as it would become known after one of its more famous practitioners. Instead he moved here, first to a house in Royal Hospital Road in 1861, then on to 101 Cheyne Walk in 1863 and to 96 Cheyne Walk in 1866, where he would live for a further eleven years, before moving round the corner to the White House on Tite Street.

After his bankruptcy and libel trial in 1878-9 he spent more time in Europe and lived in Paris before returning to London in the 1890s and then spending his final two years back on Cheyne Walk at number 74, dying there in 1903.

The funeral of this man who in his day had been regarded as brilliant, arrogant, litigious and aggressive, "the little bantam of Battersea Reach", but was now merely the 'grand old man' of the British art establishment, took place at Chelsea Old Church. Almost immediately a subscription scheme for a fitting memorial opened and in 1904 the French sculptor Rodin was commissioned to create it. Fifteen years later Rodin was dead and the memorial was incomplete and regarded as 'unsuitable'. Whistler's reputation was waning and so the subscribers had their money returned. Second time around, the statue of Whistler by Nicholas Dimbleby, unveiled here in 2005 as a belated centenary commemoration, offers a rather more literal interpretation than Rodin's intended Winged Victory figure: Jimmy stares across towards "his" Battersea like the old artist-ham he always in part was: moustache, neck-tie, sketch book and pencil to the fore, an opera-cloaked flourish in black metal.

Come out from Battersea Bridge Gardens, turn right and cross the river over Battersea Bridge. To the east is the Albert Bridge in grey and pink and beyond it Chelsea Bridge in white. The shoreline trees of Battersea Park can be seen between them.

When Whistler was living in Chelsea in the 1870s, Battersea Bridge was the temporary outer limit of the suburbanising and monetising forces that were flowing westward along the Thames from London. By 1850 Thomas Cubitt's development of 'Stuccoville', his initial name for Pimlico, had transformed the marshy Neathouse Estate immediately to the east of Chelsea into a new middle class quarter. In 1858 the Chelsea Embankment – combining river wall, main sewer, traffic artery and public promenade – had been constructed as far west as the Royal Hospital – and would be extended further west to Battersea Bridge in 1874. It transformed the once tucked-away village of Chelsea into a more public territory. With its ornamental benches and lamp standards and the suddenly accessible river views down Battersea Reach, the Embankment offered a "coup d'oeil that would not then be surpassed by any city in Europe". At the same time the south side of the Thames was becoming opened up. Elegant new river crossings were now possible via Chelsea Bridge (1858) and the Albert Bridge (1873). As a knock-on from these Battersea Fields, the frighteningly uncontrolled open space on the Surrey side between the two bridges, long notorious for its "Sunday abominations" and "sports of the lowest and most vulgar kind", had become sanitized into a public park with gates, railings and by-laws. The new Battersea Park, 12 years in its conception, land accumulation and laying out, opened in 1858.

Battersea Bridge and Chelsea church. Etching by James Whistler, 1878/9. The image has been printed in reverse

But Battersea Bridge, built in 1771 on the site of an older ferry, still represented an earlier, less tidy and less planned version of London. The old bridge had not yet been deemed unsafe (it would close in 1883 and be replaced in 1890 by the present cast-iron bridge designed by Joseph Bazalgette). For the moment the "rude timber superstructure" of its ramshackle, multi-arched crossing could offer Whistler both subject matter and a viewing platform for his work.

To see Battersea Bridge as a boundary between an old and a new London is also a way in to understanding those locations that Whistler chose to paint and those he ignored. He etched and painted the older Thames bridges at Battersea and Putney, but did not trouble to record the recently-built ones at Chelsea or Wandsworth; he used the Chelsea Embankment as a viewing platform, but rarely painted it; he was drawn to the raffish nightlife of Cremorne Gardens as a subject, but ignored the sedate walks and newly-planted prospects of Battersea Park; he etched the vanishing shopfronts of old Chelsea, but not the stucco palaces of Pimlico. But most of all, whether from his Chelsea window, from the Embankment or from the back of Walter Greaves' skiff on the river he was drawn to the line of sooty, evil-smelling and darkly monumental factories that towered over Cheyne Walk from the Battersea side of the river.

They were as dramatic a contrast with the domestic spaces of Chelsea as an artist might hope for and they were also surprisingly recent. Twenty five years earlier when Turner had been living on Cheyne Walk, he had contrasted his 'London view', looking east from his house towards the City, with what he called his 'Dutch view' which looked west along the river towards Battersea; a prospect that in the 1840s was still relatively open and rural.

Once over Battersea Bridge, turn right down the path taking you into a brick-paved open space with a statue at its centre. Go past the statue and turn left onto the Thames Path to follow it to the west.

[An alternative route, if the tide is out and you have suitable footwear, is to cross Battersea Bridge Road and take the steps on the other side of the bridge down to the river foreshore. Turn left to pass back under the bridge and follow the foreshore for 600 metres. Re-join the Thames

Path at the public slipway beyond St Mary's church. The foreshore route will take you past a line of circular bronze mooring rings recessed into the river wall. These date from 1907 when the Morgans Crucible company rebuilt this stretch of the Thames embankment so it could be used for mooring their vessels. These rings are the only surviving evidence for Morgans' 115-year occupancy of this site]

Even if the supercharging of London property prices and the fetishising of riverside views have transformed the old adage of "Battersea as the new South Chelsea" from estate agents' joke into a highly leveraged reality, nevertheless the crossing of the river at this point is still freighted with a certain class anxiety. *Up the Junction* and *Poor Cow*, Nell Dunn's 1960s novels of the Battersea-Chelsea social divide, may have slipped from paperback best-seller to social history, but the old south-of-the-river stigma still lingers on here. When Francesca Grillo, a nanny working for Charles Saatchi and Nigella Lawson and living at their house in Eaton Square, went on trial in 2012 for fraud, she was quoted as saying, 'I would rather go to jail than have to live in Battersea.'

This striking divide between what had once been two very similar riverside villages, the one on the Middlesex and the other on the Surrey side, arose as a result of the enormous concentration of manufacturing industry in Battersea from the 1850s. Morgans Crucible arrived in that decade and went on to become one of the biggest and most successful of the Battersea factories. It began, as the name suggests, with crucible manufacture before expanding in the twentieth century into electrical carbon products. Morgans Advanced Materials is still a global business supplying thermal ceramics and graphite products, but no longer operates from Battersea. The factory closed in 1971 and by 1984, after excavation and back filling with new soil, the private houses of the Morgans Walk estate had been built on its de-contaminated site. It is this estate of houses which the Thames Path takes us around the edge of, starting from the small brick-paved open space with pollarded plane trees at the foot of the bridge which was the site of the former Battersea Fire Station.

Morgans began manufacturing at Battersea in 1856 when the five Morgan brothers set up their Patent Plumbago Manufacturing Company. Crucibles had been in use since the Bronze Age for all forms of metal making from fine jewellery through to large-scale smelting. Until Morgans came along they had been made of fired clay and had a short life. But with the addition of graphite (known as 'plumbago', a stable crystalline form of carbon close to coal), the heat-refractive properties of the amalgam produced crucibles that were more durable and less prone to cracking. Starting up in what had been a disused porcelain factory and shipping raw graphite in from Sri Lanka (previously Ceylon), the brothers' innovation paid off and their *Salamander* brand crucibles (a mythical beast believed to live in fire) became a commercial success. Extending from their first factory in 1862, the company, now renamed as Morgans Crucible, expanded inexorably along the riverside, taking over saw mills, chemical works, steam boat dockyards and a sugar factory over the next 60 years. By 1920 their 11 acre site extended from Battersea Bridge almost to Battersea church and was employing over 4000 people.

If incorporating graphite into crucibles was the initial innovation, then subsequent developments took the same raw materials and used them to create new products for the emerging electrical industry. Morgans went on to manufacture carbon brushes for electric motors, carbon rods for arc lighting and carbon filaments for electrical resistors.

The rods that provided the intense light source for cinema projectors in the 1920s and 1930s would then become the light source for searchlight manufacture in the 1940s. But it was the war that proved the beginning of the end for Morgans at Battersea. As a company manufacturing military materials they were required to set up 'shadow' factories away from London and the threat of bombing. Post-war it was these shadow tails that began to wag the Battersea dog. The factories at Norton (for carbon brushes), at Tamworth (for crucibles) and then in 1947 at Neston in the Wirral and at Jarrow became the main places of manufacture. The 1956 Clean Air Act was a further disincentive and the last of the polluting carbon brush manufacture was shifted to Swansea, leaving Battersea as just the rump of a head office and research centre.

Whistler had first looked out upon Morgans' works when he moved to his new house at 101 Cheyne Walk in 1863. Almost immediately he began to incorporate it into one of his earliest and most famous London paintings. *The Balcony*, begun in the year that he moved to Cheyne Walk, still has a strangeness about it that must, when first exhibited, have seemed almost wilful. In the foreground a group of young women dressed in fashionable Japanese costume pose beneath the green sun blinds of Whistler's balcony. But filling the background, seen from high up across the river and framed through its frieze of kimono-ed mannequins and a spray of flowers, is Morgans factory smouldering sootily in the sunshine.

This startling juxtaposition – the *japonisme* chic of bright young costumed things, done in broad brush strokes with a disorienting lack of detail, set against dirty factory chimneys and mounds of graphite – has still not lost its eerie strangeness, but there is a further oddity about the picture. Equally striking is the way that Whistler's view chooses to look south from Chelsea to Battersea. Rather than treating the south bank of the Thames as a mere viewing platform for metropolitan magnificence (think of Hollar's surveys of the City of London, Wordsworth's musing on Westminster Bridge or Monet's framings of the Houses of Parliament). Whistler had reversed the view and focused on an un-regarded part of London. One gets a sense of the alien and un-pictorial nature of Battersea riverside from another source: steamers had recently opened up the Thames to day-trippers and the regular sailings from London to destinations like Richmond and Hampton Court had quickly generated their own supporting tourism literature. The disparaging advice about this stretch of the river can be taken as the metropolitan consensus: "a succession of factories...unwholesome looking swamps, yards and quays and wagon-sheds, auxiliaries to the manufactories of gin, soap, starch, silk, paper, candles, beer and vitriol".

But where Halls *Guidebook to the River Thames* found "only objects that blot the landscape", Whistler deliberately, almost perversely, found a new landscape. By bringing the brooding frontage of Morgans and other Battersea factories into his canvases, initially as backdrop but then increasingly as the focus of his work, Whistler was embarked on something quite radical. As his friend Walford Graham Robertson later put it, "his vison is that of one who has seen something that man has looked at for centuries, and never seen before". Through the 1870s as he developed his new style of 'nocturne' painting, Whistler repeatedly painted Morgans' factory at twilight, turning it into a succession of studies of light, colour and tonality. After Morgans capped off their new Italianate six-storey office building in 1872 with an illuminated clock tower (known locally as 'Ted Morgans' Folly') this landmark came to pervade Whistlers' later paintings. Its beacon of yellow light becomes the only certain point in an otherwise shifting twilit riverscape: 'Ces sites d'atmosphère et d'eau s'étendaient a l'infini' as the French critic and novelist Huysmans described them. Whistler himself could sense the metamorphosis that was taking place, "the poor buildings lose themselves in the dim sky, and the warehouses are palaces in the night".

Battersea and Battersea bridge. Etching by Walter Greaves, n.d. Greaves not only worked as Whistler's boatman but learned his own technique as an artist from him

When Morgans closed its Battesea factory in 1971 the end-game was messy and contentious. There was a great deal of local opposition to their proposals for a high rise office development on the site and they further antagonised some local people with their clumsy response to a community mural which the artist Brian Barnes and the Wandsworth Mural Workshop had painted on the factory wall by way of a protest at the plans. Contractors came at dawn and demolished most of the wall, Barnes then painted a riposte on the remaining stretch and the saga of the 'Morgans Wall' has gone on to secure an honourable place in local agitprop history. Meanwhile the planning refusals continued; it took fourteen years for the site to be rebuilt by which time the office tower blocks got whittled down to the low-rise brick domesticity of Morgans Walk as seen today. In 1981 planning permission for 226 family flats was granted, but was conditional on Morgans creating a public riverside path. Wates then built the four-storey estate. Compared to what awaits further down the Thames Path, these brick-built houses now feel safely domestic and almost modestly vernacular, but at the time their redevelopment was seen as hugely significant in terms of what was to come.

First of all, the company's successful extrication from Battersea's riverfront and the redevelopment of their industrial site, slow and painful though it was, would provide a template for neighbouring businesses. Over the next fifteen years Rank Hovis McDougal, Prices, Gartons and a host of smaller players would each cash in their land assets and head for the exit, creating in the process larger-scale redevelopments on their vacated sites. Secondly the redevelopment of the Morgans factory led to the creation of one of the very first sections of what is now the Thames Path. The LCC and the successor GLC had long-nurtured plans for river-side industry to relocate out of London and for their sites to become housing. As part of that process they wanted to create a public path along the Thames. In 1969 The GLC came up with a proposal for a river path to run from Battersea Bridge just as far as Battersea church. The closure of Morgans in 1971 made this possible and, with the completion of Morgans Walk by 1984, it became a reality.

Today the Thames Path, with its long vistas, appears to suggest a river that has always been open and accessible. It is easy to forget just how startlingly recent a conception this is, and difficult too to re-imagine that older private river front with its lines of separate businesses, each sealed off with their patented mysteries and closed to view. When Whistler painted the Morgans works or etched Prices candle factory in the 1870s he could only obtain his views from a hired boat or from the opposite bank. Even twenty years ago most of this stretch of the riverside was still separate wharves and factories. The high walls, iron-bound gates and the time clocks have given way to subtler entry points guarded by cctv, touch-pads and video entry screens. The slightly awkward paradox is that the owners of the newer developments secretly yearn for that older model and would much rather they too had remained private spaces. Instead they have been obliged to participate in the creation of a new piece of public realm as part of the deal for their own planning consent.

'Battersea Dawn' View looking from Cadogan pier to Battersea Bridge and Morgans' factory. Etching by James Whistler, 1863. The image has been printed in reverse

Continue along the Thames Path to the Monte Vetro building

The tonal shift from the brown brick of Morgans Walk to the steel grey frames and galvanised fences of the Monte Vetro site is striking enough, but this is nothing compared to the spatial shift from 4 storey horizontal to 20 storey vertical. The size and positioning of Richard Rogers' undeniably and unavoidably striking glass and steel construction owe much to the previous industrial use of its site. St Mary's, Battersea's parish church, standing next to it on the river's curve, occupies one of the most stunning points along the Thames. Yet for over two and a quarter centuries it has been shadowed by higher neighbours, of which Monte Vetro is merely the most recent and the highest. In 1788 a horizontal air mill was the first of many structures to dwarf St Mary's suddenly modest spire and it has never been able to regain its stature. The air mill morphed from wind power to steam in the 1830s and was then demolished and replaced by a succession of larger industrial buildings: the four-storey brick-built Battersea Flour Mills, also known as Mayhew's Mills, of the early twentieth century and then the yet taller grain silos of what became Rank Hovis McDougall, who closed their operations here in 1992.

When the air mill was first constructed it had required the demolition of much of the seventeenth century Bolingbroke House, built by the St John family on the site of the medieval Battersea manor house. The surviving parts were incorporated into the mill, providing the living quarters for the miller. For its first twenty years the mill ground linseed for oil and paints, which provides a quirky link with Whistler. The air mill switched to grinding corn and malt in 1808, but the oil and colour works it had supplied with linseed oil remained at Battersea. Sixty years on the impecunious Whistler used to despatch the ever-obliging Walter Greaves – bag-carrier as well as boat man – across the river to buy his master's oils and colours more cheaply from the factory gate. Greaves may have patronized Freemans varnish and colour works next door to Morgans or else Foot and Co., pigment manufacturers, beyond St Mary's church. Which means, rather whimsically, that Whistler's nocturnes of the Battersea river front must include somewhere within their twilight mysteries the very factory from which the oils used to create the paintings were manufactured.

Equally associative and of much interest to nineteenth century local historians, was the putative Battersea connection between the poet Alexander Pope and Henry St John, Viscount Bolingbroke. Bolingbroke, who had been born and would die in the family house at Battersea, had been an important political figure under Queen Anne but had fallen out of favour and gone into exile under George I, not least for his support for the Jacobite cause. By the 1730s Bolingbroke was back in England and was one of Pope's patrons. The poet frequently stayed with him and wrote much of his longer poem, *An Essay on Man*, at Bolingbroke's house. Richard Phillips in his 1817 *A Morning's Walk from London to Kew* was the first to suggest that Bolingbroke House was where Pope had worked at his poem. He got his information from Mr. Hodgson, the then Battersea miller, who assured him that "this had always been called "Pope's room... I often smoke my pipe in Mr. Pope's parlour, and think of him with due respect as I walk the part of the terrace opposite his room". From this it was but a step for various historians and Victorian compilers of topographical dictionaries to claim that Bolingbroke House "was the favourite resort of Pope, who ... composed some of his celebrated works, in a parlour wainscoted with cedar, overlooking the Thames." It is a fiction that has long been exploded; in the 1730s Bolingbroke was actually living at his house at Dawley near Uxbridge and it was there that Pope stayed, but its mythical afterlife continues to populate the internet. More's the pity: Bolingbroke's house and Pope's cedar-wainscotted parlour lie beneath the Glass Mountain's 103 apartments, so if Pope had composed *An Essay on Man* here, then it would have been hard to resist quoting from its fourth epistle:

> *Oh sons of earth! Attempt ye still to rise,*
> *By mountains piled on mountains to the skies?*
> *Heav'n still with laughter the vain toil surveys,*
> *And buries madmen in the heaps they raise.*

The height and bulk of these early industrial outriders was certainly helpful to Monte Vetro's developers as they provided precedents that could be used as to justify the immense scale of the proposal to replace, in their words, "an undistinguished and functionally obsolete industrial area" with "luxury apartment living overlooking the Thames". In the process the building managed to "flout all existing height and density restrictions and planning guidelines". Is the use of an Italian name mere linguistic marketing *impasto*? One can admire the building's careful positioning – so that all the apartments benefit from morning and evening sun; one can note how the gradations in its height – from 4-storeys adjacent to St Mary's to its 20 storey summit – mitigate some of the effects of its scale on its neighbour. But, however one cuts it, Monte Vetro is still most defiantly a glass mountain and one whose midday shadow reaches out to darken boats moored in the middle of the river.

Walk past Monte Vetro and into St Mary's churchyard. If the church is open then do go inside.

Some of the memorials inside St Mary's, including those of the St John family, pre-date the rebuilding of the church in the 1770s. The more recent late-twentieth century stained glass windows celebrate more famous yet more tangential historical figures who passed by: the poet and artist William Blake who came for the day to marry his Battersea wife but never returned; William Curtis, the Lambeth botanist, who gathered wild flowers in the church yard; and the artist J M Turner, whose view from his house on Cheyne Walk down Battersea Reach to the church must have inspired some of his final drawings and who, so the story maintains, would visit St Mary's to sketch from the vestry room, whose oriel window offers magnificent views of the Thames. If and when Turner did visit, he would have been rowed out here by Charles Greaves, the father of Walter, Whistler's boatman.

Another of the recent stained glass commissions was perhaps a little more self-serving. The memorial window to Morgans with its (punning?) image of the *Plumbago Capensis* was installed just as the company's contested proposals for redeveloping their closed factory were awaiting their planning permission. The wording on the window "to commemorate a long association with the parish of Battersea" was added just as that association was ceasing.

The churchyard encircled by established trees, the pleasingly ramshackle boat moorings and the public slipway beyond them, combine to create what feels like an interlude in an older, less-monitored and surveillance-free riverside. But to either side the admonitions start up. The notices about cctv surveillance and loitering are attached to the walls and to high wire fences, laid out in an accessible font size on a visible background colour, polite yet insistent.

St Mary's Battersea and the horizontal air mill. Engraving, 1806

Turn left off the path at Vicarage Gardens, a small planted open space

It is worth pausing to reflect on Archer House. Set back from the Thames Path behind the small public gardens on Vicarage Crescent, its angled site still has impressive part-views across the river to the north and the northwest. Yet it is a block of council flats and one of the Metropolitan Borough of Battersea's first schemes for providing houses for the working classes. This the largest block of the St John's Estate which was built by Battersea after the St Johns Training College closed. Old Battersea House, further down Vicarage Gardens, was the home of John Lefebvre a minister in government in the 1830s, who lived in the house before it became a college.

The old Metropolitan Borough of Battersea motto *Non mihi, non, tibi, sed nobis* ('Not for me, not for you, but for us') seen on the plaque high above the high arch of the entrance to Archer House reads like a reproach to everything that has since succeeded it: a jaunty and almost jarring note among the architectural solipsism that surrounds it. For surely this building takes us back to Battersea's radical political tradition, now vanished along with the factories and their organised labour which provided its grass roots? It takes us back to the Social Democratic Federation, Battersea Trades Council and the Socialist Party, to politicians such as John Burns (who first worked as an apprentice in Prices candle factory down the river), Charlotte Despard and Shapurji Saklatvala (North Battersea's Communist MP in the 1920s), and of course to John Archer himself, Saklatvala's supporter, London's first black mayor, President of the African Progress Union – and the man whose death the year before in 1932 had prompted the naming of the block of flats that we stand before.

The plaque and the architecture may suggest that municipal socialist legacy, but the reality is quite different. In 1979 Wandsworth's recently-elected Conservative administration decided to trial a new model of refurbishment for the St Johns Estate using privatisation. The existing tenants were uninterested or unable to come up with the money so the council sold the estate to Regalian Homes who by 1982 had converted its dwellings into attractively refurbished and landscaped and now relatively upmarket gated blocks of flats. None of the council tenants 'chose' to purchase a flat in what was henceforth to be called the "Battersea Village" estate. The old council motto still stands proudly on the wall, but above what has become an object lesson in local government social and economic engineering; not so much *non mihi* as 'me, me, me'.

Back on the Thames Path beyond Archer House, the tidy yellow-brick houses of Albion Quay have been laid out next to the Oyster Marina with an oblique view to the Cremorne railway bridge. They occupy the site of what was once the South London breakers yard of choice for film makers. It was here in 1968 that Jean-Luc Godard shot large chunks of *Sympathy for the Devil*, setting his pantomime Black Panthers and 'white chicks' between the stacks of rusting scrapped cars, to intone mantras of black power and wave their guns as the trains rumbled over the Thames behind them. The rusting cars were still there in 1986 when Neil Jordan filmed *Mona Lisa*. The same trains clanking over the same bridge are audible from the caravan perched on the river wall where Robbie Coltrane's Thomas and Bob Hoskins' George drink their cups of tea before stepping out into the Battersea twilight to look across the river.

Continue along the Thames Path, turning left immediately before the railway bridge and then turn right onto Lombard Road to pass under the bridge and continue past Lombard Wharf before turning right to return to the Thames Path.

The blue-painted Cremorne railway bridge is now the oldest structure apart from St Mary's church along this stretch of the river between Battersea and Wandsworth bridges. It was constructed in 1863 as part of the link line between Clapham Junction and Willesden Junction, providing the cross river interchange between the London & Brighton and the London & South-Western railway companies at Clapham and with the Great Western and London and North-Western lines at Willesden.

Just past the 18-storey four-towered blue ceramic-clad polyhedron that is the Falcon Wharf hotel and apartment building, there is another surprisingly untouched interlude. Just in front of the apron pad of the London Heliport a line of maple trees edges a small scruffy inlet where cormorants perch on the piers to digest and dry their wings, and where the wagtails coexist happily with the half-submerged lorry tires on the low-tide beach.

Turn left and then right and right along Bridges Court to detour around the Heliport and the Crowne Plaza / Altura Tower before re-joining the Thames Path

The London Heliport, which opened in 1959, was originally owned and run by Westland, the helicopter manufacturer. The land had previously been part of the eastern half of the Prices Candles factory site and it was sold off by its then owners (a triumvirate of oil companies: Shell, BP and Burmah) as a piece of rationalisation and asset-stripping when they closed down Price's own oil refining business.

The diversion around the heliport is a further reminder of the older territoriality of the river and of the time when there was no public path along its bank. It is no coincidence that Whistler's works depicting Battersea were all taken from the Chelsea side: either from public spaces such as the embankment, Battersea Bridge or Cremorne Gardens, from the balcony of his own house, or from the back of Walter Greaves' skiff in the middle of the river. There were no other viewpoints then available.

Continue along the Thames Path past the Bridges Court development to Prices Court

The competing developer/architect partnerships along the riverfront have worked hard to grab our attention, but when every building aspires to 'landmark' status, the effect can become reductive and wearying. From having been a zone that was both uniformly industrial and uniformly uniform in its appearance, Battersea has morphed into a landscape that is now uniformly residential and yet neurotically anxious to amaze.

Look carefully and one can still make out the underlying territorialities and the ancient boundaries between these new parcels of development, which generally mirror older patterns of tenures. Between the 'jelly-mould' curves of Bridges Court and the restrained yellow brick and pseudo stucco of Prices Court lies a more substantial division than mere architectural style. The visual clue is the small piece of ornamental water (with its duck-house and dogwood and hazel planting) between the two developments. Otherwise one might miss the fact that it is here that the Thames Path is crossing the old line of Battersea Creek – the mouth of the Falcon Brook and a tributary of the Thames – which joined the main river here. The Falcon Brook still rises in Streatham and Tooting and flows north, albeit underground, through Balham to skirt Clapham, but its waters no longer join the Thames as its flow was abstracted and incorporated into London's main drainage and intercepting sewer system in the 1860s. Battersea Creek remained as a piece of open water and was used by Prices as a working dock into the twentieth century.

In the medieval period the bridge that had been constructed here over the creek of the Falcon Brook was a significant enough structure to give its name to the neighbouring estate of Brug or Brugge (meaning 'bridge') and it descends to us as the current name Bridges Court. By the early nineteenth century the brook delineated the boundary between the York House estate to the west (the medieval London home of the Archbishop of York had been constructed here in 1460) and Sherwood Lodge, a more recent Regency mansion and grounds, to the east. By 1850 both had fallen from their earlier grandeur. York House briefly became the manufactory for Battersea enamels in the eighteenth century, then a chemical works making 'oil of vitriol' (Sulphuric Acid) before turning into a private lunatic asylum. Its acquisition, demolition and rebuilding by Prices in 1856 (along with Sherwood Lodge) was just the latest step-change in a decline from archiepiscopal palace to candle factory.

Prices had begun as a small candle factory on a riverside corner of the York House estate before 1840 and then, with the commercial success of their new stearine candles and the closure of their main factory by Vauxhall Bridge, had expanded from their Battersea toehold to acquire both York House and Sherwood Lodge. Battersea Creek now ran through the middle of their factory and provided mooring space for the barges bringing in raw materials (initially coconut and palm oil then paraffin wax) and shipping out the finished products.

In the same way that Morgans had moved from being a small company with one innovative product to a global manufacturer for the electrical industries, so too Prices, who started by using the industrial chemistry of saponification to create inexpensive but technically superior stearine candles, responded to the discovery of oil in Burma and North America by adapting their candle manufacture to use paraffin wax and to make themselves into a global brand. It would take another 30 years and the development of the internal combustion engine for a use to be found for one of the more explosive by-products of the oil they refined into paraffin wax but, pending that moment, and as the candle market shrank, Prices doubled up as an oil refinery, producing lubricating and engine oils alongside its nightlights and candles.

Morgans and Prices ended up as the two biggest businesses and the two largest employers in Battersea and there are other similarities between them. Both began as small family concerns run by brothers who consciously switched from commerce into manufacture; both succeeded initially through startling technological and material innovations that exploited colonial raw materials from the same island of Ceylon, now Sri Lanka: coconut oil for candles and graphite for crucibles. Both adapted to new technologies and developed new by-products to dominate in their respective fields. Both then rapidly exited from Battersea at the end of the twentieth century, selling up their factory estates for housing. Strangest of all, given their once imposing presence here, both have vanished almost without trace.

Turn left down York Place and walk down to York Road

York Place, previously 'Silk Factory Lane' from an earlier industrial structure, is where the only evidence for Prices 170 year presence can be found. Prices sold its river frontage for redevelopment in 1998 and shifted its main manufacture out to a new factory unit in Bicester. However it continued its hand candle making operation here for a further three years in the small group of its 1860s factory buildings on the corner of York Road. With their exaggerated and extended metal mansard roofs, these were preserved and converted by Wimpey into 'Candlemakers Apartments' in 2001. Next to them on York Place the lower curved-roofed building was the factory entrance lodge where the workers would clock on. Originally all of the Prices factory buildings lining the river had this same signature curved roof. Their outlines can be seen in the etching that Whistler made of the factory in the late 1870s. Continuing left onto York Road one other Prices building, the former wholesale candle shop, has survived. Until recently this traded as Charles Farris Candles (a West London church candle makers that Prices had taken over and made one of their brands); it now sells mainly fine furniture and interior design.

Prices factory seen from the Thames. Photograph after 1856

Return back down York Place and turn left onto the Thames Path and continue beyond Prices Court to Plantation Wharf

In the early 1870s Whistler began to adopt musical terms to describe his new paintings. The first of his twilight paintings of Battersea and the Thames had been called "moonlights", but now he decided they were to be called "nocturnes" in an allusion to the solo piano pieces composed by Chopin. He renamed other works too: *The Balcony*, his earliest view of Morgans, became *Variations in Flesh Colour and*

Green while the 1863 portrait of his mistress, Jo Heffernan, metamorphosed into *Symphony in White: No. 1*. Subsequently he gave all his portraits and landscapes musical titles.

In doing this he was engaging with the fashionable and emerging theory of what we now call Synaesthesia – the notion that an art form operating within one sense (say, painting and sight) might also stimulate another different sense (perhaps, music and hearing). Cultural figures like the critic Walter Pater were associated with the theory and Algernon Swinburne, Whistler's friend and Chelsea neighbour, was experimenting with a similar approach in his poetry. He composed a poem reflecting on and specifically to be exhibited with Whistler's *Symphony in White: No. 1* as well as writing a number of 'Nocturne' poems. As Whistler was to argue at his libel trial against Ruskin in 1878, "Music is the poetry of sound; Painting is the poetry of sight". Elsewhere he defined his increasingly un-anecdotal and un-figurative nocturne paintings as arrangements of line and form. Expanding on this idea, he argued "Why should not I call my paintings, symphonies, arrangements, harmonies, nocturnes & so forth?"

For these late-nineteenth century artists it was the fusion between the two senses of sight and sound that was the area for experimentation. None of them yet sought to engage with the sense of smell and we have had to wait until the twenty first century for the emergence of 'olfactory art' as a concept. It may not have existed when Whistler was active here, but as much as any other sense, it was smell that came to define the factories of Battersea. Indeed, what had become known by the 1970s as "the Battersea smell" was a powerful, distinctive and extremely disagreeable stink (variously compared to the decay of dead bodies and to the odour of rotting animal feet) that hung in particular over the stretch of Battersea riverfront now occupied by Plantation Wharf.

The culprits were the two glucose and starch factories. Gartons had come to a five acre site here in 1882, taking over the former 'Silk Factory' site that was by then used for woollens and glove making. They produced starch, glucose syrups from maize and saccharum from cane sugar. Both the latter were used for brewing and distilling (and in 1900 Richard Garton was also chairman of the London brewers Watneys). During the war they also went on to produce penicillin. The western half of the Plantation Wharf site towards Wandsworth Bridge was occupied by the other starch manufacturer, Orlandos. It was Gartons who, in developing cattle feed manufactured from the waste-products left over from their corn and rice starch production, were responsible for the poisonously particular "Battersea smell".

That heady stink from Gartons (easily triumphing over Battersea's competing cocktail of paraffin wax, ammonia, petroleum, malt, turpentine, distilling, sulphuric acid and sugar) has given way since 1985 to the blue and pink brick PoMo of Plantation Wharf. With its faux-balconies, stick-on gables and high-arched colonial warehouse chic, it appears to be alluding to some altogether different and olfactorily-neutral industrial history. The names given to its various 'Rows' and blocks: Calico, Cocoa, Cotton, Molasses and Ivory suggest sweeter smelling and visually more agreeable products than the synesthetic reality of what was once here.

A post marking the boundary between Battersea parish and Wandsworth (rendered purposeless when the two boroughs merged in 1965) used to stand on the river's edge just beyond Plantation Wharf. Now it is just one more unacknowledged point among the sweep of newer and taller buildings and regenerated 'quarters' (Battersea Reach, Riverside West, Imperial Wharf) that continue their tidal surge up-river beyond Wandsworth Bridge. Nevertheless it feels like an appropriate place to stop walking.

It was Whistler who had suggested, when talking of his nocturne paintings, that the warehouses and factories of Battersea had been transformed into 'palaces in the night'. What can one say of the transformation of these same spaces wrought by more recent re-developments? Deyan Sudjic has described the process as "tooth and claw laissez faire urbanism". Perhaps that in offering 'palatial' balconied flats with views along 'Whistler's Reach' on an industrial scale, stacked high and not sold cheap, they have created a new version of the Victorian warehouse building for the twenty first century.

To return to Chelsea either retrace your steps or continue along the Thames Path and cross the Thames by Wandsworth Bridge and return along the Kings Road.

Whistler's paintings and etchings

Etching was one of Whistler's favoured mediums. His London series of etched views made along the Thames in 1863 gave him his first breakthrough as an artist and it was in that series that he first came to record Battersea. The plate 'Battersea Dawn' was made from Cadogan Pier, where the Albert Bridge would later cross the Thames, looking south west to the factories of Battersea.

The two great virtues of etching were their immediacy and their portability. The work was executed on small prepared copper plates using a needle, both of which Whistler could carry in his pocket. Coming upon an old Chelsea shop-front, or seeing Prices' candle works from the back of Walter Greaves' boat, he could rapidly etch the view with an almost photographic immediacy. "Certain truths, certain beauties, certain swift relations between the thrilled observer and the fleeting beam of light" was how the painter Walter Sickert (another of Whistler's apprentices) would later describe Whistler's etching technique.

The great disadvantage of etching an urban landscape (unless like William Blake did, you can teach yourself to etch in mirror) is that the impression taken from the plate, the print, is reversed. That doesn't much matter if the subject is the human face or a vase of flowers, but in Whistler's etchings of London, Paris or Venice the viewer is required to mentally reverse (or simply ignore) the relationships between the buildings. Perhaps more people were going to notice the transposition of San Giorgio Maggiore and Santa Maria del Salute in his Venice series than were going to spot that Chelsea church is on the wrong side of the river or that his view from Cadogan pier to Battersea Bridge and Morgans looks the wrong way. But Whistler's etchings require reversing if they are to be used as a visual record of place.

By contrast, while the etchings were instant *jeux d'esprit* to be knocked off in situ, Whistler's nocturnes were done more carefully and executed in the studio from recollection long after the event. He had received training in visual memory when he was in Paris in the 1850s. This had taught him to absorb and memorise the salient details of a subject and to transfer them on the canvas later. Sickert recalled walks with him along the Thames when Whistler would stop and "look for about ten minutes at a given subject, isolating it as much as possible from its surroundings". He would then turn his back and recall the scene, "There is a tavern window, three panes wide, one each side of the central partition and six panes deep. On the left is a red curtain half-drawn... The tone of the roof is darker than that of the wall, but is warm in colour and precisely the same value as is the sky behind it which is a deep blue-grey". It was from such forays along the Chelsea Embankment or out on the twilight river seated in the back of Greaves' boat, that he assembled the memories and the outlines of Battersea that fed into his series of nocturnes. Sometimes, as Greaves recalled, he would make simple sketches using white chalk on brown paper to help set out the composition, "just showing the position of the lights and the river banks and the bridges"

Tate Britain has four of Whistler's nocturnes: *Battersea Bridge, Cremorne Lights, Nocturne in Black and Gold: The Firewheel and Nocturne in Blue and Silver – Chelsea.* However, anyone wishing to view those of his paintings which show the Morgans factory has to be prepared to travel. *The Balcony* and *Nocturne in Blue and Silver – Battersea Reach* are both in the Freer Gallery; and while you are in Washington you might as well catch another nocturne of Morgans in the Corcoran and the one hanging on the wall of the White House. A further *Nocturne in Blue and Silver* showing Morgans is in the collection at Yale; others are in Paris, Detroit and Glasgow.

Acknowledgements

Cover design and map taken from Stanford's map of London, 1862.

Illustrations credits:
p 4	Jon Newman
pp 9, 14 & 16	Kensington and Chelsea Local Studies Collection
p 20	Lambeth Archives
p 26	Wandsworth Heritage Centre

Thanks to Sean Creighton for reading and commenting on the text, to the staff at Wandsworth Heritage Centre and Kensington and Chelsea Local Studies collection for their help, and to all the Crowdfunder supporters and Arts Council England for their financial assistance.

GOING FURTHER

If this walk booklet has left you wanting to find out more about James Whistler then there are a number of ways in to his work. The best collections of his paintings in the UK are found first in the Hunterian Art Gallery in Glasgow and then in Tate Britain, London; however the majority of his works depicting Battersea are in US galleries. A good collection of his etchings is also held by the Ashmolean Museum in Oxford. There are a number of biographies of Whistler; Daniel E Sutherland's *Whistler: A Life for Art's Sake* is one of the more recent; *An American in London: Whistler and the Thames* by Margaret F. MacDonald and Patricia de Montfort is the catalogue to the 2013 Dulwich Picture Gallery exhibition and offers a good way in to the artist's London works.